FOURTH WORLD WOMAN

poems by

Lara Gularte

Finishing Line Press
Georgetown, Kentucky

FOURTH WORLD WOMAN

Publisher: Leah Huete de Maines
Editor: Christen Kincaid
Cover Art: Pamela Findleton, pamelafindleton.com
          and Ashley Bennett Stoddard, ashleybennettstoddard.com
Author Photo: Brian Chapman
Cover Design: Elizabeth Maines McCleavy

Order online: www.finishinglinepress.com
          also available on amazon.com

Author inquiries and mail orders:
Finishing Line Press
P. O. Box 1626
Georgetown, Kentucky 40324
U. S. A.

Table of Contents

To the memory of Al Young, California Poet Laureate, 2005-2008

Our time on this Earth may be ending, but I have enjoyed looking at clouds—

—Dana Levin

PART I

In the depth of winter, I finally learned within me,
there lay an invincible summer.
—Albert Camus

THE BITTERNESS OF TEA

She hides secrets from herself,
in the teapot trimmed in gold leaf.

Dried lavender, mildew, and old spores
hover and haunt her.
She stabs a spoon into murky leaves.

In the teapot she sees her reflection,
remembers the pure brew of her past.

Steam releases silhouettes from the spout,
and vapors bring the windows to tears.

Cup of Chai with a little honey and mint leaves,
a holy swallowing.

She sees faces on plates of almond cookies,
ánd her lips turn to sugar lumps.

Slicing a lemon, she slices herself.
Her blood spills thick.

Everything red before turning to Earl Grey.

LEAVES

I long for those birds,
clouds of ducks and geese
their flight home
myself bound to earth,
to these mountains.

I watch leaves
drop
one by one,
the distance between now
and my future shortens.

This November, dappled
with drizzle and dropped clouds.
It's the leaves that fill me,
the damp that gnaws
the long merging shadows.

I believe what thunder says,
see with my own eyes
the spaces between the leaves
fill with light.

THE CLOSE SKY

She waits for the test to come back negative
while death leans into the side of the house.
Nothing between her and the sky but the window.
The evening star shivers,
clouds move by, covering the brightness.

Her face at the open pane, half here and half there—
where her mother ghosts among the trees.
She falls from the dormer. Her soul shatters,
she divides into parts,
absorbing the rush of every piece back inside her.

Outside in the night the Barred Owl circles,
and everything closes in.
She knows she should run.
Her face reflecting the star's light
tangled in her hair.

If ANGELS ARE MESSENGERS

The morning sky, slate gray. Snow swallows the house, seals the doors. The woodstove empty, my life casts off little heat. Snowflakes press their damp wings against the window. An angel in a gauzy, sleeveless dress beats at the glass.

I let her inside. Snow melts from her body. A scent of narcissus infuses the air. Grounded for centuries the celestial being regrets the dull weight of mortality, blames her human past for the fall.

She tells me to beware of lights flickering at the tunnel's end, and warning about the deceptive sun, advises me to stay indoors, lie down on my pillow, dream of flight.

When a light bulb bursts, the house becomes a cold inferno. The seraph turns whiter at the center of a flame. Her face cracks, her smile curls inward, all her ashes collapse.

TRANSCENDING MY DAYLIGHT BODY

The cat finds the sock
stuffed inside my surgical bra,
runs away with it.
My body, a long stocking of desire.

Above my missing breast,
a tiny crucifix.

I pray for a holy flame
against my chest,
a miracle of uncut tissue,
nipples pressed against silk.

A dove flies in the window
and I'm immaculate,
a full moon,
two breasts filled with cream.

Suddenly there's heat on my shoulder
soft as down.

HER FATE LINKED TO THE SUN'S DECLINE

She wants to return to the time of fullness—
only the gravid moon, egg filled.

Yolks bump against moonshell to breaking,
spill through cumulous clouds.

The night shines on her through the window.
10,000 bats rise from the eaves.

In fractured starlight, red clots of eyes peer at her
from a constellation of broken spirits.

She becomes transparent,
curls in the circle of a new moon.

Gravity pulls on her,
stars break apart in her head.

The morning's weak sun
can't burn away her bad dream.

BEWARE OF BIRDS THAT STRIKE
FROM DARK PLACES

In a world of bones,
    dark birds scream and plunge.

Sky ragged with shadow,
    every leaf on the oak an apparition,

bare twigs point toward the earth
    in warning.

Red tail circles the meadow,
    hovers on air and light—

balance act with wind,
    the swoon and the dip, wings fall.

Beak and pinions descend,
    pitched cry of hunger—

the dive for flesh,
    talons into soft tissue.

The rabbit squirms
    under the heart of the hawk's body.

Sudden tearing of air, branches wave, light bends,
    the cottontail lifted out of life.

Pierce and tear of sharp beak,
    steam of incarnation,

chest opens to the four-chambered core,
    hear the pounding, the search for breath.

MY FISH STORY

The river that drew me here threads through the mountain, a thin line of existence. I lean over the current, lift a net of dark weight. A giant fish shape swallows me when I pull it from the water. Inside fish belly my skin peels away, exposes the black flapping thing within me. I pray for a river rat to gnaw me free, hope that the shore will fill my arms when I reach out. The next day, among leaf rot and silt, wet newspapers lie on the river bank, covered in fish scales.

THE YEAR SHE LOST HER WHEREABOUTS

She travels the path of the glacier
carrying the world with her.

A blizzard claws her,
and she turns her knife to a mountain cat's throat.

To repent for the kill, she prays, asks for favors,
hears angels howl like wolves.

Seen from a distance a field of them,
wings folded into fur.

The seraphs drool of moon
stroke her with their paws.

Snow covers her, and she sleeps,
waits for the season of warming.

Time passes till she steps out of snow melt,
staggers among carrion and crags, downed limbs,

comes upon birds not heard from for years
who cross clouds like borders.

Something final has begun
with nothing she can do to stop it.

BEAUTY

Tender inside, like the pulp of a fruit,
my body celebrates its losses

with still life on the table;
a cut melon, pink and ripe,
a dead dove on a china plate.

I lift the bird from Blue Willow,
place it aloft, a soft weight in the air,
where it can come alive again,
flail its wings, contest with the wind.

Deception necessary,
I drape my body in satin.

When I turn to pose,
the sky is birdless.
Soft fabric drops from my shoulder.

Students sketch with one eye closed,
my one left breast.

Fill in the rest of me with ochre.

WHERE THE HIGHWAY LEADS

One hoof, one paw, after another,

    a trail of footprints
    departing out of the chain.

Archaic in the modern world,

    the forgotten tethered mare,
    the poisoned polliwog,
    the abused dog's rage.

No happy tongues or tails,

    only animals that hide
    in the back room of the pet store.

Ants swarm the lab mouse's body,

    a procession of pieces taking new life.

Orderly cattle in chutes,

    the screams
    of the parts of them we have eaten.

These parts trapped inside of us

    while we rev idling motors
    moving herdlike, nose to tail,
    where the highway leads
    searching for a savage and simple life.

CALIFORNIA'S GOLDEN HILLS

The looting of trees by October winds
lightning strikes dry grass
wires down and sparking.

Screaming wind gusts make trails in the air
for fire to travel.

Roads enter fleeing people,
unwind down the center of their lives.
Shadows run from soul-burning by red smoke.

The extinct, brown bear bellows
from the voice of an old woman.

Those too close to the heat and nowhere to fall
ascend into air a fiery lightness of being.

When the rains come
a survivor with singed beard
in a yellow slicker
shovels seed into sod.

WHERE THE DOVES GO

I see them fly en masse—
soar, dip, whirl.
On mission, they send messages,
and the sky goes to coo.

These peaceniks have known another world,
pulsate between stars,
gleam in the freezing night.

They slip into downy warmth,
face forces of wind and ice.
Wings cover the sky.

In their descent,
darkness falls on their flight of faith,
and they find hail on the dove cote roof.
White birds on frayed phone wire hang on hope.

With the smell of burning feathers—
no peaceful ascent.
All eternity earthbound.

These days I'm a wingless bird
struggling to take flight,
condor on my shoulder.

THESE STONES

After the "Camp Fire" Paradise Pines, California

I follow behind a backhoe, see the burnt scarring,
a desolate landscape of ash heaps, vanished lives.

In a vacant lot of cinder, I remember my mother's Camellia tree,
how she liked Gerbera daisies, my grandmother's tea rose.

Granite binds me to this property, the stones
my uncle gave to my father, to stabilize the embankment.

I choose to believe something still breathes here.
When I call out, I hear a heartbeat.

Fierce rocks pull away from the ground,
and I remember who I am.

These stones on the hillside cover a stubborn root,
a long vein, blood of my blood, alive deep inside.

In the passage of my remaining days I'm here to survive myself,
grow wings to fly through smoke.

DREAMING THE AMERICAN RIVER

She begins in still water, heart suspended.
Gray rain shines, around her.

Over rock bed she flows, crests, and troughs,
tastes the savory, cold broth.

Carried along the curving storm,
water fatigued she gulps the sky.

To current she yields, her limbs like oars.
Around her the silky weight of fish roil and plunge.

Dashed to rocks, river rushes blood gush.
Her wounds soothed by the cold stream.

Rapids deliver her to the river mouth
where the waters call geese down.

In the mud and shallows of her dreams
the weak sun reveals a thin chord of rainbow light.

Her heart battered and beating, she waits for the ferryman
to travel the fin of a new world, sink into scales.

THE ASCENT

She watches July's light show
shimmering from earth
to sky,
luminous with broken promises,

Thunder tumbles into a gorge.

Impossible to think under rain clatter,
her synapses vibrate,
a snake of lightning strikes.

At the center of her brain,
the fizzle of sparks.

Her life the reflection of shadows
sticking to tree shade,
black into black.

Clap of thunder
and the choked cry of the loon.

Between conifers a new soul rises.

Near the smoking boulder
a midden of ashes,
the rattle of wings.

GRAY LODGE

Near Gridley, California

In this Pacific Flyway,
winter faith and the annual migration.

Snowstorm of geese, rising and falling,
wetlands teeming with coots, ducks, and pintails.

A flock of tundra swans fly toward the Sutter Buttes,
and the child deep inside awakens.

My eyes follow snow geese traveling to an afterlife of sky.
I slip into down warmth and my throat breaks into a honk.

I ask the air to take me far above the earth
in my own flying body

flap of wings to lift me to sky, beyond sky—
where distances don't exist

where communion of the seen
embraces the unseen

or at the moment before death
to choose rebirth or to fly.

DAY OF THE DEAD

Their voices
call from the ground,
bones rise again into the air,
dust weaves through eye sockets
and pelvic bones.

We offer them sugar candy,
sweet fruits,
scent of flowers.

They linger
at the front door,
float through windows,
lurk down hallways,
inhale candle fumes.

Lights blink on and off.

Through rooms they wander
drag a table, chairs,
across waxed floors.

They are all here,
bridge of beating pulse,
arc of blood,
to share the dark miracle.

EARTH SAVING

She scales mountains,
to call the forests and rivers back,
a return of each tree, the pure waters.

Miles of dying conifers
desperate for rain,
to escape beetle infestation.

In rock face, engraved crosses.
She remembers her house full,
no empty seats around the kitchen table.

Every day another loss, the spotted owl,
memory of songbirds covering the sky,
a beak on each tree limb.

In the arms of wind,
the moon has its teeth in her,
her shoulders too weak to hold up the world.

CLEANSING

1

Monarchs do not fly here,
nor does the yellow mustard grow.
No trees for birds to nest,
only streets
where men in long cars push
through jammed avenues.
Officials inspect wind
trapped in pillars,
examine the river
thick with lead and sludge.

2

In my home with no ceiling
I find lacework, the smell of mothballs
in my hope chest.
My grandmother weeps down
from the sky.
Tears flood my house,
swim in my ribcage,
drum on my heart.

3

All night
I feel the slippery body of water.
Seeds fall from my eyes.
In the morning I rise
with liquid hands.
When I shake them out
they turn green.
Blackbirds perch on them.

THE MOON COMES BACK FOR ME

Since my dreams stopped,
moonlight stays on the other side
of the house.

I'm in this sleep to stay.
A shroud wraps me,
I'm cold and stiff,
my mouth tastes of earth and ash.

Inside my empty hull,
a flicker—
and I blink.
Suddenly, shattered glass,
and the luminator slips
through the open window.

Host of moon, I swallow you,
discover myself in the night sky.

When they find my body,
I will rise through my skin,
my eyes will give off light.

FLIGHT OF A FLEDGLING

They travel on faith, a journey of uncertainty.
Humankind crossing through a desert brown and bleeding.

Her mami leads her by the hand till sun erases horizon,
and a large man's hands grab her, pull her into a cavern of small faces.

In this American land, her body adjusts itself under mylar,
her crucifix dropping a tear on her chest.

Rows of lost orphans curl-up where they can, shoes in a pile,
baby teeth in a box.

She sinks into dream, her mami a hummingbird,
hovering above her.

Something inside her breaths
a chest full of swallows.

In an uncertain sky she flies,
distances south, and then north—again.

CROSSINGS

The Monarch flies from México
in a sliver of sunlight.

Alert and calm,
coyote trots across a busy intersection.

Hungry people push themselves
along the dusty road.

Trails radiate animal auras,
tufts of hair.

Scorpions, lizards,
cling to rock face.

Geese leave what they know,
rush to routes of migration.

Carrier Pigeons return with dirty feet.
They huddle together.

Iron doors sweep shut,
after entry to the gated community.

A woman travels light
with her backpack,

desperate to move on
before the borders close.

PART II

If you touch the leaf deeply enough, it is eternal, deathless.

Thich Nhat Hanh

HER FATHER'S FATHER'S HUNTING KNIFE

She flees to the Sierras,
driven into exile by conditions of dystopian leanings.

She wants distance from cities where people live turbulent and teeming,
far from prophets on street corners soothsaying the end of days.

Like a big animal she lumbers up flanks of mountains,
a falcon hood conceals her identity.

She wraps a dead Peregrine in leaves, carries the bird with her,
thinks about how animals live in the moment.

On a dying planet she ascends the highest peak to become the eagle.
Against silence she screams, her voice ricocheting off igneous rocks.

To live or die against heartache and loss—
the chasms of her life, the breakdown and crumble.

She tells God she is coming with geese that fly in formation,
to die on the wing.

The wind like a fist in her chest,
opens old wounds, scar tissue protects her heart.

She plunges the hunting knife into stone
till the blade turns molten, becomes the sun.

She feels the rush, the resurrection.

ANIMAL DREAMING

"I think I could turn and live with the animals"
Walt Whitman, "Song of Myself," Verse 32

In my dream a wild sound in my head,
I cling to a horse's mane,
explore an ancient trail.

I see them springing from caverns,
crouching on a berm,
hiding behind oaks.

They crawl from beneath rocks,
rise from the field's flesh,
assemble in the meadow.

In my chest the claw digs its way out.
With a winter's slow heart,
I journey solid, heavy footed, enter a womb cave.

In fat slumber, body full of honey
breath slows,
tongue and teeth of cell memory.

Asleep till the thaw, then hunger,
my throat opens,
a growl rises up with longing.

The wolf comes to my window.
He touches the glass with his big teeth.
His jaws want me.

In the end will I survive
to collect his bones.

THE SEEING

for Stan Padilla, artist

whose eyes shine indigo,
messenger bringer, dream keeper
of the obsidian mirror.

She gazes into the dark stone
her face turns to wax.
She melts into essence of blue.

Borderless sky of azure, of cobalt.
To become the light, she tells herself to breathe.
Communion of the seen, the unseen, of luminous wings.

Reflector mirror of who she is, who she will be.
Not the predator looking forward,
but the bird, an eye on each side.

At daybreak, wings,
and she's Raven-wise.

THE NEW DARK AGES

Over a landscape of divisions,
she loses her way,
passes the hard lines of coffins.

A mask for protection from bad airs,
she searches for green space, light of day.

Sad sounding coo call of the mourning dove,
a music without mercy.

Downed by fever,
she burns into the atmosphere, breath spent.

Radiantly delirious—
she reaches out to a beaked plague doctor,
in black brimmed hat, wood cane pointing at her.

Face up to the firmament, to the heart of a cold moon,
wind moves clouds, reveals footprints for her to follow.

TENSION OF WING AND FOOT

He's marooned by weak ankles, flat feet,
unable to leap from one peak to another.

In this land of the missing—
a visionary sees the future underfoot.

Beneath the Blue Oak a new kind of moss grows.
From gravestones the long hair of the dead

tangle the living, pull them into fertile soil.
Atop a mound, slippers wait for him.

Clouds break into a sky of old shoes.
Angels fall, wings sprung from their pinions.

The sound of ruffling feathers,
talons stuck in the mud.

He hears footsteps, looks down,
his feet in combat boots.

SHE, WITHOUT A HOME

among people who live nowhere,
in her suitcase, mylar, a tin cup, and old letters.

She takes her own hand, leads herself around Sactown—
roams roads, spends days looking through trash cans,
lets the wind and rain have their way with her,

find her on B Street amid layers of refuse,
plastic bags and broken bottles.

She's without a home in this republic,
stateless in a bad economy of love and liberty.
Her world of bungalow, gate and garden gone,

a feral woman in a lost migration,
her life of shelter, food, and warm hearth, a holy memory.

Sky white with winter, she suffers migratory bird grief,
grows arm feathers, rises skyward—
a tired swallow on a long flight to find home.

DREAMING THE END OF DAYS

In a befouled earth
the living die without pity,
come alive again in another shape.

Blending of humans and beasts,
hooves and holsters.
Bodies moving, skin and fur touching.

Crow cry, fish flurry—
man, of manatee,
wolverine woman.

Nose and snout, hand and paw,
trail of animal tracks,
and footprints.

A man howls—
wonders who will be his next meal,
grabs the weak, the young, into his jaws.

Newborns with fins
emerge from the polluted river.
Moths big as pigeons.

A Sand Hill Crane loses her bearings,
flies into the night sky
till she can't sense where she's going.

A SHORT DISTANCE

I walk this crust of earth
where crestlines of buttes buckle
spilling trees and red oxides,
where I let stones wear me away.

In this canyon,
twisted arms and oaks stretch wide,
and the sandstone cliff face
holds the last light beyond the rim.

Like a Buddha
the moon floats down
piercing the dark skull
between the worlds.

Before I descend, I watch shadows change,
and a pattern of sun and night
slide across the steep mountains.
Wind stirs up the past to a chant in real time.

When my feet can't feel the ground,
the distance calms my mind.
Rocks exposed, embedded,
appear suspended,
as if floating somewhere.

TRAVELLING MY YARD DURING TIMES OF PANDEMIC

Under a lowering sky,
light shifts through tree branches,
pierces deep shade.

A gravid doe under the Blue Oak.

The emergence from amniotic shell,
placenta of plenty, the breath, the bleating,

a coming of life,
spotted, tawny, long legged.

To stay on the bough,
a moment of union with doe and fawn.

Beyond dark days,
my heart fed with divine immunity.

WOMAN OF THE QUERCUS

"Bios Urn changes the way people see death,
converting the 'end of life' into a transformation
and a return to life through nature."
                    Teodora Zareva

Among oaks and conifers, she seeks
the afterlife,
lays herself down with ancient ones.

Through the body's chambers
skin and vertebrae tremble,
blood spills, enters the heartwood.

She opens her hands wide, reaches
to a dangerous blue.
The sun lowers its head to meet her.

Arms grow branches,
from the skin of her palms, leaves grow.
Her feet press into earth.

Changed to wood,
all root, bark, and branch,
she steps out of herself in leaf.

As the last light of sun
slips through her,
she looks to the pine,

the spruce, and the cedar—
for others who chose
tree life in the hereafter.

CRACK IN THE ROOF

She sees footprints in the sky,
a shining on ceiling space,
an incandescence.

In her sleep, too many hawks in the air.
One bird of carrion flies between her dreams,
perches on her limbs.
Her heart beats double time,
her hope runs chill.

The long night carries shapes and shadows,
creatures of her imaginings, their fur and antlers glow.
Windows rattle as the wolf enters her heartwood
unleashes the claw and tooth of memory
and her stray part howls.

She searches for luminosity on the walls
sees the disembodied aglow.
A star on the ceiling shimmers,
she waits for the moon to tip,
spill light on her.

In the end she's stark naked with wings,
her bones are piccolos.
She reaches up, away from the world,
to the celestial city.
There's an afterlife;
she saw heaven as a young girl.
The moon throws down a rope for her to climb.

AFTER THE END TIMES

The hour of darkness, dirt in her eyes, pulse distant, she travels earthen tunnels,
the sod roof of the mole who rests deep in his room.

Beneath the ground, an underworld where rocks and bones are equal.

Endless night turns under the mole—
ghosts of the gone time, memories sunken into long years of loss.

Inside a raccoon carcass, a dark wing.

Deep down, still breathing, she evolves her higher self—
waits for eruption, the earth's waste to spill,

reveal germinating seeds spurred into living above ground,
seed heads opening to light.

TRAVELLING OAXACA

In this land of fantasmas, city of plazas and zocalo,
I enter the courtyard of Casa Panchita,
hear birdsong of the Primavera*,
my room among Jacaranda and Bougainvillea.

Sitting on a bench in Parque Llano
my hand smells of the street dog I fed
my last piece of bread.
His eyes follow me, his cold nose pokes my hand.

Even the pigeons think I have crumbs.
They flap their wings, they converge, they coo,
then fly off when I wave my arms to celebrate
the emptiness I will fill with this bright day.

In my travels I search for weavers,
follow the clack-clack of the loom,
find men with Indigo thread.

I circle the plaza, walk down Morelos,
find hidden shops of fine artisans,
hear cathedral bells cover pigeon talk,
the voices of saints.

In the Rufino Tamayo museum,
a Zapotec warrior contemplates defeat.
Nearby, a goddess with stone breasts.

Roaming in Zaachila
I meet a lost angel named José.
He hovers over the poor, the forgotten dogs,
then wanders the cemetery.

Back at Casa Panchita,
I listen to rain fall in the courtyard,
hear seeds snapping in wet soil.
My body like an unearthed new stone.

* Primavera is what the locals call, "The Rufous-Backed Thrush."

MONTE ALBAN, OAXACA

1.

Stone steps too steep, too narrow for her feet.
Beneath the grasses, talk of clouds that no longer exist.

She follows the path of high stone, of ancient plateau ruins,
ceremonial site of temples, palaces, steles.

Fields of bodies, necropolis of tombs and mausoleums,
architecture, open spaces, tied to the galaxy.

They vanished at the edge of a constellation,
to survive mankind's history.

2.

The ball court, oblong of grass,
granite steps on each side.

Zapotecs say the game's not about rivalry,
more like a ritual ballet of life and death.

No winners or losers,
movements in synch with moon and stars.

3.

When twilight comes,
the lunar orb, like a mirror, reveals centuries of stone.

A shadow invades the ball court,
and the earth tips away from the sun.
She looks toward far-off galaxies
to find glow from old stars.

Into the black night she rises,
hangs in the sky, a silver disc.

TO DREAM A WAY STATION

Her life lifted, dropped on a foreign coastline,
no borders from land to sea.

Under a gray whale of sky, the sea greets her as a refugee,
her past in a suitcase among snapshots.

Where she comes from, the temple in ruins,
and a die-for-freedom event.

The sea overflows fish men with big lips.
They slide limply onto shore,

seeking refuge from that place
where the Kraken swims.

In a secret language of exile,
she speaks to the fin men with a long exhale.

When darkness comes, weary stars lose their glow,
over an exhausted earth.

HOW THE BODY SURVIVES WHEN
THE LIGHT IS FAILING

The parched earth in its orbiting decay, an endless falling
of the living into turbid waters.

The still lake, heavy with the sweet scent of rot, black oil,
sweat of mercury, litter of wings, dull glint of a bluegill corpse.

She glides through a mat of broken insects,
finds herself tangled among legs and antennae.

Something iridescent swirls in her cupped hands,
delivers cold wings.

She imagines another life, the self-inside
flexing to muscle out.

Suddenly a mosquito enters her,
proboscis sharp as a hypodermic needle.

Her body turns cold, translucent,
bones, tissue, vertebrae, alchemize.

The dead intertwine her body like a vine,
pull her under.

In the deep she finds sanctuary from dystopia,
kissed by an aquatic frog.

THE CROSSING

All those years muddled
inside herself,
till her fear vanishes.

She lies suspended
in the dark
between wakefulness
and dream

where she begins
to understand
how near life
is to death,

how everything
sooner or later,
crosses over.

A prayer warms her mouth.
Birds fly across the sky
of her mirror.
Her shadow
wanders the room.

She used to think
her house had a ghost,
footsteps on the stairs,
the creaking door.

The ghost was her,
the imagined shadow
of herself.

In the morning,
what dream?
She endured the night.

She steps back
out of herself
and sees
where her footprints
turn and walk the other way.

COELACANTH

The Paleozoic ocean returns,
and water sparks leap into air.
Hypnotized by glistening surf,
she kicks off her sandals,
lunges into a mysterious ebb.

Cold currents move in her.
She crawls up sandy shallows
into the mercy of sunlight,
a creature evolving.

The earth too bright, too dry,
shore covered with skeletal crabs,
the grief of toxic turtle eggs.

Gasping, she discovers not what she is,
but what she has never been.

Out of breath,
gills and fins develop.
Her bubble eyes glow, blinded
by the sun's dazzle.

Caught in a rip current,
carried away into a dark abyss,
the deepest part of her
extinct, but alive.

FOURTH WORLD WOMAN

A fugitive of the modern world, she's tired of deep lies,
and anthems, the marble limbs of statues on the ground.
When smoky skies erase mountains and eagles,
shroud angry riots in town,
she craves the peace of forest creatures.

Imagining a fourth world the rustle of wild grass beguiles her.
The animal inside teaches her to have visions, to watch for signs.
Night moves through her, breathes and stretches,
a cold nose touching her.
She snatches the mouse from the cat's mouth, sets it free.

Antlers shadow the sky and she hurts a beautiful pain.
She molts her former selves for a furred face, nostrils slanting.
At the crest she stands doe-like, hooves in place,
awaits the deluge to cleanse the ailing earth.

ACKNOWLEDGEMENTS

I would like to thank, friend and mentor, Paul B. Roth, for his long-standing artistic support of my writing. Thank you, Red Fox Poets of the Sierra Foothills, Arts and Culture of El Dorado, Diniz Borges, director of Portuguese Beyond Borders Institute, and all the artists, poets and writers of Escritores del Nuevo Sol. Thank you Alan Soldofsky, Vamberto Freitas and Calder Lowe for your encouragement and promotion of my work.

Grateful acknowledgment is made to the following publications in which poems from collection first appeared, sometimes in a slightly different form.

Anacua Literary Arts Journal: "Flight of the Fledgling;"
The Bitter Oleander: "The Close Sky," "My Fish Story," "Coelacanth," "If Angels Are Messengers," "Her Father's Father's Hunting Knife," "Animal Dreaming," "Beware of Birds that Strike From Dark Places," "How The Body Survives When The Light Is Failing," "Dreaming the American River," "Her Fate Linked To The Sun's Decline," "The Moon Comes Back For Me," "Dreaming The End of Days," "After The End Times," "Crack In the Roof," "After the End Times," "California's Golden Hills;"
Convergerncejournal.com: "Travelling Oaxaca;"
St. Petersburg Review: "The Bitterness Of Tea;"
The Fourth River: "Leaves;"
Lake Effect: "Transcending My Daylight Body;"
January Review: "Where the Doves Go," "The Year She Lost Her Whereabouts," "Fourth World Woman;"
The Bhubanerwar Review, Online Journal of Contemporary Literature: "Tension of Wing and Foot," "Monte Alban, Oaxaca;"
Manzanita's Writer's Press: "A Short Distance;"
The Sandhill Review: "Beauty;"
Watershed: "Cleansing;"
The Sutterville Review: "Woman of the Quercus;"
Clackamas Literary Review: "The Crossing;"
California ___ Water: A Climate Crisis Anthology: "These Stones;"
___ "___ng;"
Arts Magazine: "The Ascent;"
Gaia's Lament: A Call to Awaken: "She Without a Home,"

___iew: "Where the Highway Leads."
2013, La Bloga, On-line Floricanto. "Crossings,"

Lara Gularte lives and writes in the Sierra Foothills of California. She is El Dorado County Poet Laureate 2021-2023. Her book of poetry, *Kissing the Bee*, was published by The Bitter Oleander Press, in 2018. Nominated for several Pushcart Prizes, Gularte has been published in national and international journals and anthologies. Her poetry depicting her Azorean heritage is included in the *The Gávea-Brown Book of Portuguese-American Poetry*, and in *Writers of the Portuguese Diaspora in the United States and Canada*. She is affiliated with the *Cagarro Colloquium: Azorian Diaspora Writers, at the Portuguese Beyond Borders Institute (PBBI), California State University-Fresno*. In 2017 Gularte traveled to Cuba with a delegation of American poets and presented her poetry at the Festival Internacional de Poesia de la Habana. She's a proud member of the esteemed, "Escritores Del Nuevo Sol." Gularte is a creative writing instructor for Arts in Corrections at Mule Creek prison.

www.ingramcontent.com/pod-product-compliance
Lightning Source LLC
Chambersburg PA
CBHW021204090426
42740CB00008B/1229